HISTORY ENCYCLOPEDIA

WORLD WAR I

An imprint of Om Books International

Contents

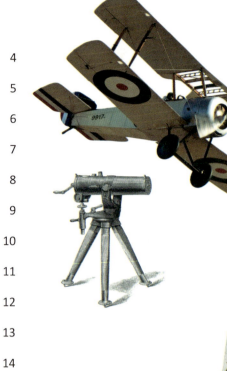

Strategy of the Western Allies	4
The German Invasion	5
Battle of Marne	6
Austria Invades Serbia	7
World War I Taken to the Seas	8
The Submarine War of Germany	9
Treaty of London	10
Germany Suffers Huge Losses	11
US Enters World War I	12
Peace Move by the United States	13
The 14-Point Declaration	14
Russian Revolution of 1917	16
China Sides Up with the Allies in World War I	17
World War I Takes to the Skies	18
Collapse of Austria and Hungary	19
The Allies Emerge Victorious	20
End of the German War	22
The Terms of the Armistice	23
World War I and the Destruction Left in its Wake	24
The Axis and the Allies	25
Outbreak of World War II	26
World War II Weaponry	27
Russo-Finnish War	28
Hitler's Role in World War II	29
Hitler's Views on Race	30
Invasion of Norway	31
The German Attack	32

WORLD WAR I

1914–1918

The Austro-Hungarian Empire was ruled by the Hapsburg dynasty. Serbia, a country south of the Austria–Hungary border, was an ally of the Russia Empire . The Austro-Hungarian powers were looking for an excuse to enter into a war with Serbia. The assassination of Archduke Ferdinand was looked upon as a personal offence and as an attack made to the entire country. It was soon believed that Serbia was behind the attack, even if it was the work of Serbian nationalists acting independently. The Austro-Hungarian powers declared an unreasonable ultimatum to Serbia. They agreed to most of the points but refused two: that unnamed Serbian officials should be dismissed as per the request of Austro-Hungarian military and that there should be Austro-Hungarian participation in movements against them in the Serbian soil.

An event that had begun as a local European war soon gathered momentum and became a global war that extended for four long years from 1914 to 1918. World War I became the first war wherein 28 nation states from around the world were involved. It was no wonder then that it gained the name The Great War or the war to end all wars.

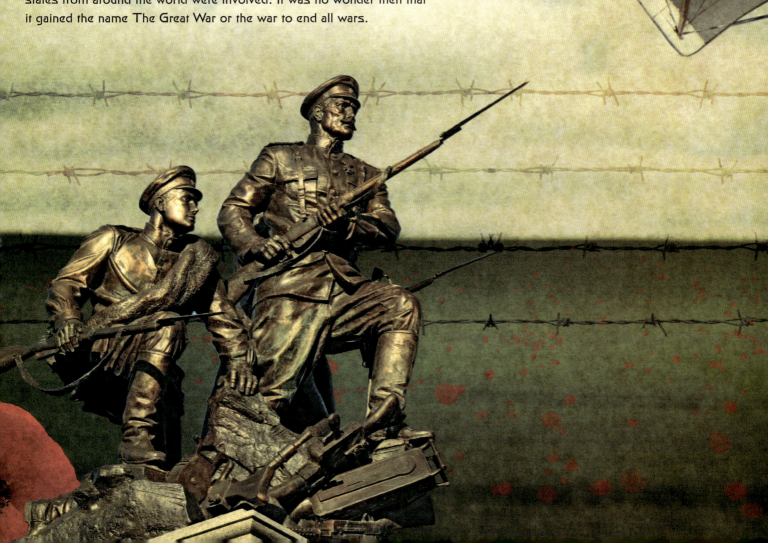

HISTORY ENCYCLOPEDIA

Strategy of the Western Allies

German infantry advancing during manoeuvres.

France decided to take on the offensive strategy and attack Germany before it was completely ready for it. Hence, General J Joffre, the chief of General Staff came up with the Plan XVII. This was a mobilisation plan. But it underrated the German force and wrongly undervalued the German army deployment thinking that the Germans would deploy only 68 infantry divisions, when in reality the Germans actually deployed 83 infantry divisions.

Plan XVII

According to Plan XVII, the French would attack from different places and await the response of the German troops. They would defend themselves and continue to resist the attack until their ally Russia could join and support their side of the attacks. The plan included the segregation of troops in different regions. The first army was supposed to have attacked from Alsace, while the second army would attack the German troops in Lorraine.

Attack via Belgium

Joseph Joffre, one of the men behind Plan XVII, did not take into the account the possibility of a German invasion of France via Belgium. They realised this only some time before the declaration of the war but it was too late to re-strategise. The French believed that Germany would want to avoid British involvement. So they believed that Germany would not invade via Belgium, especially since Britain had a neutrality treaty with Belgium at the time. Even after the French were able to correctly estimate the German armies' strength, they lacked faith in their own troops.

Defeat of the French armies

The attack of the German troops in Alsace-Lorraine by the French failed miserably. There were heavy losses caused by miscalculation and lack of proper available weapons. The same was the case in Belgium where the preparedness and available artillery for warfare was lesser than in Lorraine. The French suffered massive losses and were pushed back to their starting points. Germany managed to move into Belgium and the northern part of France to a point only a few kilometres from Paris. However, they were unable to do much here as by this point the German troops were losing their supplies and feeling fatigued.

Helmuth von Moltke the Younger led the Marne Campaign for the Germans.

FAST FACT

The First Battle of Marne was fought once the retreating French troops reached their destination and received reinforcements from the French and British armies.

World War I Germans medal Iron Cross.

German invaders of Belgium came in long trains of supplies, such as these horse-drawn field kitchens.

4

The German Invasion

The Germans had to work towards reducing the effect of the Liege Fortress which protected Belgium. German troops crossed the frontier into Belgium and later Brussels with their 420 mm siege guns.

Battle of the Frontiers

The Frontier battles were fought on the French-German border in Alsace-Lorraine and the French-Belgian border in north-eastern France. Seven Imperial German Army contingents moved towards the west as per a carefully laid out plan, under Germany's tactical Schlieffen Plan. The Germans did not foresee such stiff resistance from the Belgian and French troops. The French plan was to have an offensive operation on Germany's eastern border and also on the north-eastern Franco-Belgian border of the Ardennes region. At the declaration of war between Germany and France, the French army moved towards both directions to battle the German troops. There were four major battles in the Battles of the Frontiers. They included, the Battle of Lorraine, the Battle of the Ardennes, the Battle of Charleroi and the Battle of Mons.

The largest battle

The Battle of the Frontiers was the largest battle of the war. At the time, it was declared the largest battle of human history as more than two million soldiers were involved in the battle. The German imperial princes commanded armies in Lorraine. Crown Prince Rupert of Bavaria sent his sixth army as a counter-attack before the French advance was successful. Crown Prince William of Germany also sent his army.

Charge of the "Ninth Lancers" during the "Great Retreat" from Mons to Cambrai attacking a German battery of 11 guns.

The impact of the battle

The Battle of the Marne was the very large and visible wound caused by the offensive attacks and counter-attacks taken on by both nations. The Germans deployed about 50 per cent more troops than the French. Joffre's Plan XVII collapsed, but he quickly came up with a new plan and stationed a newly created sixth army to the north of Paris. Germans moved away from the original plan by Schlieffen due to Moltke's indecisiveness and also bad communication between his headquarters and field army commanders. It is said that Moltke can be blamed for Germany's losses.

Heavily armed German soldiers advancing in Belgium.

German soldiers strain to move a huge siege gun into an attack position. The massive gun was designed shortly before World War I, to defeat the strongest fortifications such as those at Liege, Belgium.

Battle of Marne

The first Battle of Marne started in September 1914. It was started by the French army and the British Forces against the Germans, who had occupied Belgium and were very close to invading Paris. Within a few weeks, it seemed as if the German Schlieffen plan was falling apart and it had faced great resistance from Belgium.

FAST FACT
The Parisian taxis used to help move troops quickly around the battlefield came to be known as "taxis of the Marne". They were seen as an icon of France's determination to win the war.

French troops equipped for battle at a train station possibly during the Battle of the Marne.

How the battle was fought?

Belgium had managed to get more soldiers contrary to the German expectations. Germany needed to mobilise more men immediately, which they failed to do, while Russia managed to get together more men. This is why the battle of Marne was fought near the River Marne. It is believed that Moltke, distracted by the losses at the site of the German offensive in Lorrain had not issued orders to the first, second and third armies deployed for the Battle of Marine. Allegedly, after the German retreat, Moltke had announced that the Germans had lost the war.

Exhausted troops

After the outbreak of the war, Germans had advanced into France and the French troops were fatigued after their retreat towards the Marne River which had lasted for more than 10 days. General Joseph Joffre took a risk with a counterattack and the allies exploited certain gaps within the German troops and sent the French troops in.

The surprise attack

Some 6,000 infantrymen were transported from Paris in 600 taxis. It was the first time that automotive transport of troops had happened in the history of war. This surprise night attack resulted in German retreat.

A model of the taxi of Marne.

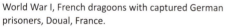

World War I, French dragoons with captured German prisoners, Douai, France.

The 33 m tall Memorial of Mondement commemorates the French victory of the Marne as well as the soldiers who protected France.

Austria Invades Serbia

After Archduke Ferdinand's assassination, a small period of diplomatic strategy was initiated between Austria-Hungary, Germany, Russia, France and Britain. It is now known as the "July Crisis". Austria-Hungary in its quest to finish the Serbian intrusion within Bosnia gave the state a series of 10 demands of which 8 were approved by Serbia.

Austro-Hungarian soldiers by the statue of Karađorđe in Belgrade in 1915. It was destroyed by the Austro-Hungarian government.

U-14, an Austro-Hungarian submarine was launched in 1912 as the French Brumaire-class submarine. During the war, she was captured and rebuilt for service by the Austro-Hungarian Navy.

First Austrian invasion

Austro-Hungary declared war on Siberia 28th July, 1914. The first Austrian invasion of Serbia began with a very small number of troops, but was quickly thwarted by the Serbian commander, Radomir Putnik. Austrians began a second attack against the Serbs on the Drina River.

Battle of the Kolubara

The Battle of Kolubara, also known as the "Battle of Suvobor", remained one of the most important battles that were fought between the Serbian and the Austro-Hungarian armies during World War I.

Both sides wanted to capture the Serbian capital of Belgrade. Between November and December 1914, there had been some fighting that had raged on in the 200 km long stretch from Belgrade to Guča and had brought the Serbian army to a situation of complete collapse. However, they managed to take over the First Army and took over against the well-equipped Austrian army. The Austro-Hungarians captured the city and entered the capital as conquerors. Nevertheless, the battle had led to great loss of soldiers on both sides. The Serbs launched a massive counter-attack on December 2 and the unprepared Austro-Hungarians were taken aback at the quick Serbian response. By 6th December, the Austro-Hungarian defences collapsed with many soldiers abandoning their weapons and becoming Serbian prisoners. The third Austrian attack was successful to a certain extent in the Battle of the Kolubara. Serbians were forced to withdraw from Belgrade, but a Serbian counterattack took back Belgrade which forced the Austrians to retreat.

Fort Sommo used from the Austro-Hungarian army during World War I.

Uniforms of the Austro-Hungarian Army.

HISTORY ENCYCLOPEDIA

World War I Taken to the Seas

German U-boat's torpedo passes the stern of a British vessel

At the start of the war, USA tried to get the British and German sides to agree to the Declaration of London. Even though Germany agreed, England did not. She did not want to give up her advantage. So, the German submarines trailed the waters near England and sank the ships carrying supplies.

Old bronze sextant used for navigation.

Where was the war fought?

World War I was largely fought on land, but the sea was used to equip the Allies with both resources and manpower that helped them continue their armed assault. There were times when the Germans attacked British fleets. This led to great damage especially in the Battle of Jutland in 1916. This battle was also called the largest clash of battleships. Even then the Germans were unable to gain the upper hand on the seas although the successful attacks by German U-boats managed to leave some impact on the Allies. The United States joined the war owing to these attacks.

Germany stalked areas around the North Sea. Here she could control the entry and exits of ships and submarines. At the time, USA had taken a neutral stand. Germany's high-handedness angered the US, who declared war against Germany in 1917. The reason for this was that USA aimed to safeguard the seas and uphold its rights as a neutral nation.

Stalking of seas

Soon the British navy began to stalk the seas to try and stop vessels from entering Germany. Both nations began to possess illegal goods from each others attacks. The USA and England then laid down stringent laws against the attacks and procedures followed by both nations.

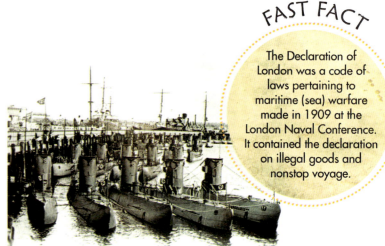

German U-boats on display.

FAST FACT

The Declaration of London was a code of laws pertaining to maritime (sea) warfare made in 1909 at the London Naval Conference. It contained the declaration on illegal goods and nonstop voyage.

The Submarine War of Germany

German submarines at Kiel, Schleswig-Holstein, on 17th February, 1914.

When World War I moved to the sea, Germany gained an upper hand with her use of submarines. At the beginning of World War I, 38 German U-boats attained prominent victories against British warships, but Germany wavered over using the U-boats on merchant ships because they anticipated a reaction from neutral countries like USA. However, in 1917, they went ahead with this plan and angered the US into joining the Allied forces and entering the war.

Use of U-boats during the war

The U-boats started sinking merchant ships that approached Britain or France. In 1917, the Germans sunk 430 allied and neutral ships. Towards the end of the war, Germany had built 334 U-boats and around 226 submarines were still under construction. The U-boats used by the German troops were fitted with 150 mm guns. The fortunes of the allied powers changed with the entry of the US in the war. At the time, the US was a major player in the shipping industry. Before the Great War, submarines were generally armed with self-propelled torpedoes that were used to attack enemy ships. During the Great War, the submarines were enhanced to have deck guns pre-fitted on the body of the submarines. The soldiers within the submarines would first approach the enemy merchant ships at a safe distance and signal them to stop. If the enemy ship pursued, they would be targeted and then sunk with the deck guns.

Germany lost its early advantage with this great response from the US. It is said that during the World War I, 60 U-boats were at sea at one time. World War I proved that despite their small size and robust build, the U-boats could be massive weapons of destruction as they destroyed tons of merchandise from hundreds of ships.

FAST FACT

German Chancellor Bethmann Hollweg was the one who announced Germany's decision to opt for unrestricted submarine warfare.

German sailors standing on the conning tower of a U-boat after torpedoing a British cargo ship.

Treaty of London

The Treaty of London is also referred to as the London Pact. It was a secret treaty whose main goal was to get Italy on the side of the Allied powers against Germany. The treaty was signed between the nations of the Triple Entente (Britain, France and Russia) and Italy. While Russia signed to protect Serbia, France and Italy signed to agree that they would not attack each other.

Treaty of London 1867.

Italy's demands

The Allied forces were very eager for neutral Italy to join their side in the First World War. The main reason for this was that Italy bordered Austria. In return for their participation, Italy demanded certain territories which it was to gain if the Allied Forces won the First World War. Italy was promised the northern part of Dalmatia, Trieste and some eight more territories. So, even though most Italians wanted to remain neutral, the government of Italy decided to join the Allied forces in the war against Austria-Hungary.

Italy's additional share

In the treaty, it was also decided that Italy would gain a share in the Mediterranean region (which lies next to the Adalia province) in the event of a partition in Turkey. Italy also demanded that they be the official representatives of Albania in its relations with Foreign Powers. Italy was promised a share of war indemnity matching to its efforts and participation. Also, Great Britain was to give Italy a loan of 5,00,00,000 pounds.

Disavowal of the treaty

At the end of World War I, Britain and France refused to meet their promises which they had made in the pact. They split up the colonial territories amongst themselves which further upset Italy. In the Paris Peace Conference, USA had urged the nations against meeting the terms of the Treaty of London as it was a secret pact. It was decided here that all nations were to keep their pacts and promises public. The Treaty of London and all of its contents were revealed to the world when it was published in a Russian journal by the Bolshevik Russian State. Italy saw the refusal of Britain and France to meet the pact as a blatant betrayal.

1915: Treaty of London is signed

1918: Pact is nullified by the Treaty of Versailles

FAST FACT

In 1918, US President Woodrow Wilson announced his "Fourteen Points" which was to be a blueprint for peace. He had prepared these points after a careful and thorough inquiry with his team of 150 advisors.

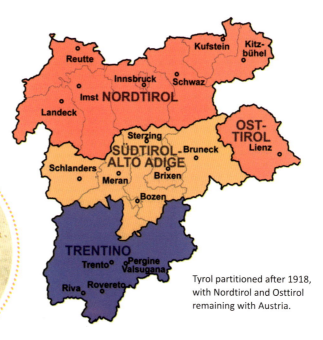

Tyrol partitioned after 1918, with Nordtirol and Osttirol remaining with Austria.

Germany Suffers Huge Losses

Togoland was a German colony in West Africa. On 5th August, 1914, Britain had declared war on Germany. Soon after, the allied parties had cut up the sea cables between Monrovia and Tenerife to weaken the radio connections between Germany and Togoland. Then, British and French troops captured and divided Togoland for themselves.

The graves of the Belgian soldiers who fought in World War I.

Operation Michael

At the start of World War I, in 1914, Amiens had been a base for the British Expeditionary Force. It was then captured by the German soldiers. The French re-captured this base. In 1918, the Germans launched a Spring Offensive called "Operation Michael". The Second Army of the Germans fought and drove away the Britain Fifth Army. On 4th April, 1918, the Germans managed to successfully capture Villers-Bretonneux, which overlooked Amiens. However, on the same night, Australian troops counter-attacked and re-captured it from the Germans. During their attempts to capture Amiens, the German troops had bombed repeatedly and created great loss to life and property. The Battle of Amiens was then launched in August, 1918 by the British Expeditionary Force. The end of this battle led to an Armistice with Germany and ended the First World War. Thus, the war ended with the German armistice and surrender to the Allies.

German prisoners in a French prison camp.

Toll of destruction

More than 40 crore soldiers from the Central and Allied forces were left injured or wounded by the war. Many of the soldiers even went missing and were never to be found again. Many civilians lost their lives as well. Many parts of the world had to be reconstructed and re-planned due to the heavy damage and destruction caused by repeated bombing and war tactics.

German economy collapses

The British navy blocked German ports, which meant that thousands of Germans were starving and the economy was collapsing. The German navy suffered a major mutiny. After Kaiser Wilhelm II abdicated on 9th November, 1918, the leaders from both sides met at Compiegne, France. The peace armistice was signed on 11th November. The Russian, Ottoman, German and Austro-Hungarian empires had collapsed because of the war.

1914: German troops attack Amiens

1918: The Battle of Amiens ends World War I

Statue of a soldier, a World War I memorial in the town of Pleneuf, France was built to commemorate victims of World War I.

HISTORY ENCYCLOPEDIA

US Enters World War I

The United States entered World War I in 1917, almost two and half years after it had started in 1914. This was because of President Wilson's policy of being neutral towards the war. However, the incident with Germany's submarines as well as the US's urge to gain world peace forced Woodrow Wilson, the Commander-in-Chief (a title earned as the President) to enter into the war and protect themselves against the attacks by the German submarines.

The American flag.

US as a moneylender

German U-boats had sunk three American merchant ships causing heavy loss of life. This was when the US declared war against Germany. The entry of the US in the war turned the tables against Germany. By 1917, the allies had exhausted their coffers by paying for essential supplies and armaments. As the US had joined the side of the Allied Forces, they made financial contributions in purchasing armaments and supplies. At this point, only the US could afford the supplies. The US made many loans to the allies from 1917 to the end of the war. These loans built up to more than seven billion dollars.

A postcard depicting Americans creeping on the Germans with hand grenades.

American Army troops parading in Scotland.

Germany as the enemy

The US also sent food to the nations and armies of the Allies. They entered the war with money and soldiers, both of which were needed desperately by all nations. The US dispatched more than 10,00,000 soldiers under the US commander General John J. Pershing. Its navy focussed on the construction of destroyers and submarine chasers to protect the allies from German U-boats. Owing to the US declaration of war against Germany, other nation states like Cuba, Panama, Haiti, Brazil, Guatemala, Nicaragua, Costa Rica and Honduras joined the war against Germany by July 1918.

1917: The US joins the Great War

1918: Costa Rica and other countries support Allies

Peace Move by the United States

Francis Joseph, Austria's emperor, died on 21st November, 1916. Charles I succeeded him as the new emperor. He wanted to initiate peace with the Allied and Central powers but this failed. Later, a German Reichstag member named Matthias Erzberger, tried to negotiate peace. His attempts were also met with failure. Another peace move was made in London by Lord Lansdowne, who suggested negotiations on the basis of the status quo antebellum, "the state existing before the war", but this was rejected. US President Woodrow Wilson became the spokesman of peace and came up with a plan called "Fourteen Points".

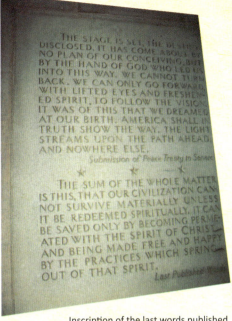

Inscription of the last words published by Woodrow Wilson on the west wall of the Wilson Bay in Washington National Cathedral.

Wilson's Fourteen Points

Woodrow Wilson's Fourteen Points asked for an open declaration of peace and the abandonment of secret diplomacy. It also asked for the freedom to navigate on the high seas during the time of war and peace as well as the freedom to trade between nations. It also asked for a definite decrease of armaments, a neutral colonial resolution obliging not only the imperial powers but also the people of their colonies, the mass departure of nations from all Russian territories and respect for Russia's right to self-determination, the complete restoration of Belgium, a total German withdrawal from France, a readjustment of Italy's borders on the basis of ethnicity, an open vision of independence for the people of Austria-Hungary, restoration of Romania, Serbia and Montenegro, with access to the sea for Serbia, the prospect of autonomy for non-Turkish people of the Ottoman Empire, a sovereign Poland with access to the sea, "a general association of nations" and to guarantee the independence and integrity of all states both great and small. Wilson's peace campaign became one of the reasons that led to the fall of the German government in October 1918.

President Woodrow Wilson (1856-1924).

William Howard Taft with the newly inaugurated President Woodrow Wilson during the inauguration ceremony on 4th March, 1913.

FAST FACT

In the Fourteen Points laid down by Woodrow Wilson and his team, the first five points dealt with matters of international concern and the next eight were to do with specific border and territorial matters.

The 14-Point Declaration

President Woodrow Wilson believed in remaining peaceful and neutral. Until the incident with Germany, he was determined to maintain a neutral stand in the World War I. Once the US entered the war from the side of the Allied Forces, President Woodrow Wilson put in many resources and a lot of money to earn a victory. After the war, he returned to the peace strategy and laid down the fourteen-point plan for peace. Other members of the Allied Forces believed the plan to be too idealistic.

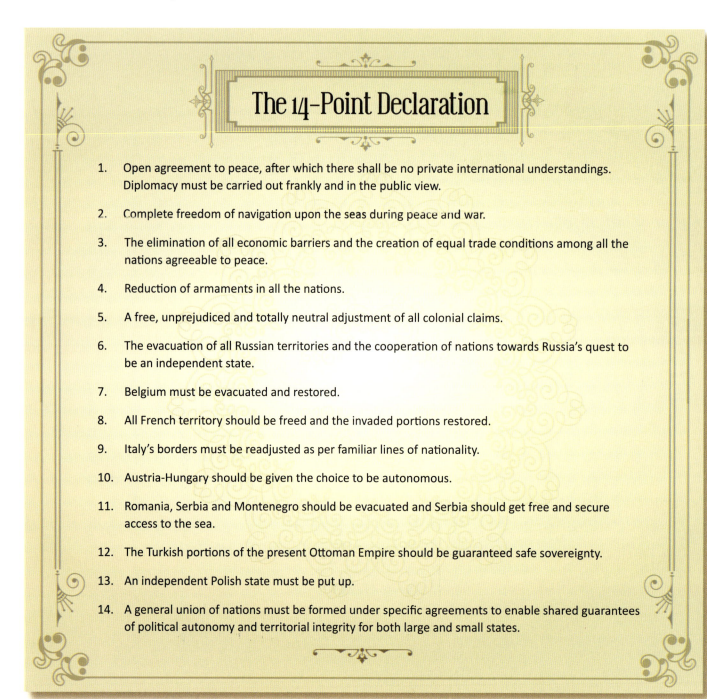

The 14-Point Declaration

1. Open agreement to peace, after which there shall be no private international understandings. Diplomacy must be carried out frankly and in the public view.
2. Complete freedom of navigation upon the seas during peace and war.
3. The elimination of all economic barriers and the creation of equal trade conditions among all the nations agreeable to peace.
4. Reduction of armaments in all the nations.
5. A free, unprejudiced and totally neutral adjustment of all colonial claims.
6. The evacuation of all Russian territories and the cooperation of nations towards Russia's quest to be an independent state.
7. Belgium must be evacuated and restored.
8. All French territory should be freed and the invaded portions restored.
9. Italy's borders must be readjusted as per familiar lines of nationality.
10. Austria-Hungary should be given the choice to be autonomous.
11. Romania, Serbia and Montenegro should be evacuated and Serbia should get free and secure access to the sea.
12. The Turkish portions of the present Ottoman Empire should be guaranteed safe sovereignty.
13. An independent Polish state must be put up.
14. A general union of nations must be formed under specific agreements to enable shared guarantees of political autonomy and territorial integrity for both large and small states.

WORLD WAR I

Woodrow Wilson (1856-1924) addressing the Congress in 1917.

> **FAST FACT**
> Johannes Bell, a German jurist, was one of the representatives from Germany who signed the Treaty of Versailles.

Objectives of the plan

US President Woodrow Wilson had outlined the objectives of US involvement in the war in his Congress speech where he used these "Fourteen Points". His points were seen as extremely idealistic and they met with resistance in the Paris Peace Conference. But it did become the foundation for Germany's surrender in November 1918. However Wilson's administration via its diplomatic channels managed to get France and Italy's support for the Fourteen Points. This campaign was part of Woodrow Wilson's discourse that with German officials. The situation, for Germany, had gone from bad to worse and this deteriorating situation ensured that they approach the Allies for help.

In 1918, when the German Chancellor Prince Maximilian of Baden, sent a note to President Wilson, requesting an immediate armistice and opening peace negotiations on the basis of the Fourteen Points.

This led to the meeting by Allied and Central Powers at Paris to discuss the Treaty of Versailles. Germany was blamed for all the destruction and devastation caused by the battles of the war. Germany felt thoroughly defeated. They were unable to defend themselves when so many powers were speaking against them. Thus, they had no other choice but to accept all the conditions put upon them by the Treaty of Versailles. They needed the help of the other powers to restore themselves as a nation.

1918: Announcement of the 14-point plan

1918: Germany signs the Treaty of Versailles

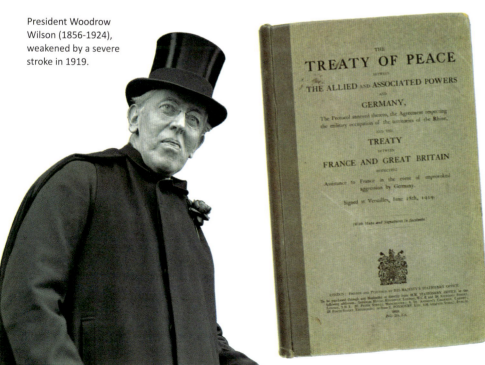

President Woodrow Wilson (1856-1924), weakened by a severe stroke in 1919.

The Treaty of Versailles was one of the peace treaties at the end of World War I. It ended the state of war between Germany and the Allied Powers.

Russian Revolution of 1917

The Russian Revolution was a movement started by the Bolshevik Party of Russia. This revolution aimed to end the Tsarist system followed in Russia and led to the formation of the Soviet Union. The Russian Empire came to an end with the abdication of Tsar Nicholas II. A temporary government was formed in February 1917 which had members of the Bolshevik Party.

Formation of a new republic

By 1916, Romania was fighting alongside Russia. By March 1917, the nationalist uproar in the Russian Empire quickly spread and there was widespread support for the efforts made by the moderate Socialist revolutionary, Aleksandr Kerensky. By April the National Moldavian Committee insisted on autonomy, land reforms and the use of the Romanian language. A move towards complete sovereignty was further pushed due to the events in Ukraine, where a council called as the "Sfat" was formed based on the model of the Kiev Rada, which proclaimed Bessarabia as an autonomous republic of the Federation of Russian Republics.

Bolshevik parade in St Petersberg during the Russian Revolution in the spring of 1917.

Military help

The Sfat appealed to the allies for military help. The Bolshevik Revolution of November 1917 put an end to the provisional government formed by the Bolshevik Party and got the Marxist Bolsheviks under the leadership of Vladimir I. Lenin came to power and put an end to Russia's contribution to the war. Acknowledging the possibility of isolation and taken aback by the affectation of the Ukrainian government, the Sfat voted for conditional union with Romania in April 1918. Reservations about the union were deserted with the defeat of the Central Powers and the creation of Greater Romania. An unconditional union was voted at the final session of the Sfat in December 1918.

A statue of Lenin.

FAST FACT

Did you know that a treaty under the Paris Peace Conference signed on 28th October, 1920 by Romania, Great Britain, France, Italy and Japan, documented the union of Bessarabia with Romania? All signatories (except Japan) finally ratified this.

Bolshevik revolution, 1917.

China Sides Up with the Allies in World War I

A bronze statue of Sun Yat-sen emplaced in the Memorial Hall in Guangzhou, China. Sun (1866-1925) was a revolutionary and political leader and the founding father of Republican China.

China soon sided up with the Allies when World War I entered its fourth year. World War I was at first limited to European nations but then began to include countries in Africa and Asia. The two competing nations, Japan and China, also had their role to play in the war. Japan was an old ally of England and had already declared war on Germany in 1914 and had captured Tsingtao, a German naval base at the Shantung Peninsula in China. After the capture of Shantung, Japan wanted direct control over Shantung, the southern parts of Manchuria and East Mongolia. It also wanted to capture the islands in the South Pacific which were under Germany's control.

Sun Yat-sen declares himself emperor

Sun Yat-sen, founder of the Kuomintang (KMT), used the anger of the Chinese people over Japan's demands and declared himself emperor. The opposition from China's military forced him to accept republican government. China declared war on Germany on 14th August 1917 to regain control over the Shantung Peninsula and to regain its power.

International delegates in the Palace des Glaces (Hall of Mirrors) during the signing of the Peace Terms ending World War I in Versailles, France.

The Paris Peace Conference

The Paris Peace Conference took place in January 1919 at Versailles and was called to put up the peace terms post the Great War. Although there were 30 different countries that participated, it was the United Kingdom, France, USA and Italy also known as the "Big Four" who became the dominant forces who were responsible for the formulation for the Treaty of Versailles, a treaty that ended World War I. During the Paris Peace Conference, the Allied Supreme Council backed Japan in its claim to control Shantung. This angered the Chinese leaders present in the peace conference.

Diplomatic meeting between the French and Chinese delegations.

World War I Takes to the Skies

While the war was fought primarily on land and sea, planes were often used to conduct survey missions. Fighting in the skies began with very minor exchanges of fire shots between these missions. It was only in 1915 that fighter aircrafts with machine guns and planned bombings of enemy air bases were initiated.

World War I aircraft in a dogfight. Britain vs Germany over the battlefields of Europe.

Planned bombing during World War I

The First World War witnessed the development of many lethal defence mechanisms and technologies including the machine gun, poison gas, flame-throwers, tanks and aircrafts. These weapons and defence technology had greater power and prowess to kill. The First World War also saw the introduction of weapons like the Big Bertha, which was a 48-tonne gun that had the capability to fire a shell over 9 km. However, it took around 200 men and many hours to assemble. Target bombing began with England's bombing of Cologne, Düsseldorf and Friedrichshafen in 1914. German aeroplanes strategically bombed Britain in the years of 1915 and 1916. England then targeted factories.

London bombed by the Germans

The air raids conducted during World War I were largely destructive and took many lives. Air raids could easily help strike at the enemy's vital resources. Most of such air raids occurred from 1914 to 1918. The East End of London became one of the most popular targets for such air raids.

England used air strikes as per the attacks from German submarines, but Germany remained steadfast in attacking the towns of England. In June 1917, Germany bombed London with 118 high-explosive bombs. These raids were taken very seriously by England. They began to look at strategic bombing with more thought and planning. German raids on Britain, for example, caused 1,413 deaths and 3,409 injuries.

FAST FACT

The first separate air service in the world "the Royal Air Force" was initiated in 1917.

Wreckage of a World War I German Albatross fighter biplane.

British two-seater monoplane fires on a World War I German Taube fighter. A rifle is used to shoot at the pilot of the German plane.

Collapse of Austria and Hungary

After World War I, Austria began to fall apart. Its leaders approached the Allied Forces and requested for peace. They ordered the retreat of the Austrian army. Austria, Hungary and Czechoslovakia split from the Austria-Hungarian Empire. Also, Ireland became an independent state and split from the United Kingdom, remaining a part of the British Empire. Yugoslavia was formed from the Kingdom of Serbia.

Cavalry Austria and Hungary.

The Black Hand

Austro-Hungary was the power whose territorial ambitions played a large part in the coming of war in 1914. Although head of an increasingly fossilised and outdated regime, the Habsburg emperor Franz Josef was an expansionist. In 1914, his latest addition to the Austro-Hungarian Empire was Bosnia-Herzegovina. Bosnian Serbs resented the Austrian rule and sought the protection of independent Serbia. It was a member of this Bosnian Serb group, the Black Hand, who had assassinated Archduke Franz Ferdinand in Sarajevo.

Austria declares war on Serbia

Austria quickly sent Serbia an ultimatum and declared war on the 28th July, 1914. A few days later, on 1st August, Germany declared war on Russia. Russians and Germans considered themselves to be the champions of the Slav people.

Law for a free state

The Czechoslovak committee in Prague passed a law for a "free state", while a parallel Polish committee in Krakow brought together Galicia and Austrian Silesia into unified Poland. Soon, the German members of the Reichsrat in Vienna announced the formation of an independent state of German Austria.

Austria surrenders

An Austrian delegation arrived in Italy to surrender unconditionally. That same day, Hungary formally declared its independence. On 3rd November, all the terms of the Austrian armistice (peace treaty) were in place and on the following day, Austria-Hungary formally ceased to exist.

Austria became the successor state of Cisleithania and the Austria-Hungarian Empire. Also, Turkey became a successor state of the Ottoman Empire. Estonia and Finland gained independence from the Russian Empire. France, Italy, Britain and Japan regained many of their old territories which were captured by the Central Forces during World War I.

German Chancellor, von Bethmann Hollweg, addressing the Reichstag during the crisis of July 1914, when the Central Powers (Austria-Hungary) and the Triple Entente initiated the World War I.

Austrian mountain troops in the Isonzo district, clinging to rocks and helping each other along by ropes. They were climbing over mountain pass to surprise an Italian detachment.

HISTORY ENCYCLOPEDIA

The Allies Emerge Victorious

Germany signed a peace treaty with the new Bolshevik government in Russia. Because of this, Germany could deploy all of its forces against the allies on its western border. But Germany was unable to succeed. The allied troops pushed back the Germans with the added strength of the American troops. The US deployed fighter planes and tanks in the Argonne Forest, which was the strongest part of the German line.

World War I, The New York Tribune, caption of illustration reads: "A Yankee Terrier Gets Its Teeth in a German Sea Wolf".

War spoils

In 1918, the Allied armies had advanced into the Western Front and soon the Germans had to abandon their naval bases on the Belgian coast. Many of its U-boats were surrendered to the Royal Navy as spoils of war. But there were many losses on both sides including human and property losses.

End of the war in sight

By September 1918, German army leaders met with German chancellor Kaiser Wilhelm and reported that they had lost the war. Wilhelm asked his foreign secretary to send a secret message to the US President Woodrow Wilson. President Wilson asked if Germany was willing to accept the peace proposals that he had offered months ago. Germany declined the proposition. At the time, German troops slowly began to run away from the army. Strikes broke out amongst the civilians. Industries refused to produce war-related goods. The Allied Forces launched the Hundred Days Offensive to crush the German opposition. Sailors of the Imperial German Navy began a mutiny and a German Revolution broke out. Which is why the German government decided to sign an armistice even though their troops were still stationed in Belgium and France. In the armistice, the Germans were asked to evacuate Luxembourg, France and Belgium with immediate effect within the next 15 days. Rhineland was to be occupied by the Allied troops.

FAST FACT

The Polish Government also faced an uprising in December of that year after the armistice which left Poland as a German concern.

Two German U-boats washed up on the rocks at Falmouth, England, in 1921. Both were sunk during World War I.

WORLD WAR I

Peace terms

The peace terms stated that Germany must withdraw its forces from all of the territories it had occupied. It had to agree to evacuate from Alsace-Lorraine and give up its weapons including airplanes, submarines and battleships. Germany was to hand over trucks, railroad engines and other supplies. The German delegation refused to sign such an agreement. But with no stable German government at the helm as Kaiser Wilhelm had resigned and fled the country, a decision had to be made. After much argument, Germany agreed to the allied terms and signed the peace treaty. The prolonged World War I brought forth an end to the imperial dynasties especially for states like Germany, Austria-Hungary and Russia.

Yanks and Tommies (British soldiers) celebrate the armistice ending of World War I.

German delegation meets the allies

A German delegation attended a meeting at the Allied military headquarters to discuss peace terms. The delegation was met by the Supreme Allied Commander, Marshal Ferdinand Foch of France who wanted Germany to officially ask for a ceasefire. Only then would the peace terms be offered to Germany. After some resistance, Germany had no other choice but to accept the armistice.

Demands from Germany

A series of battles known as the "Hundred Days Offensive" were fought and this included the battle of Amiens, the Second Battle of Somme, and many more near the Hindenburg Line. Soon the Germans were forced to retreat back to Germany. The exhausted German forces wanted an armistice to negotiate and come to terms with a peace treaty. However, there was little time and lots of pressure from the Allied forces. The internal strikes in Germany also led to a quick surrender.

1914: Start of World War I

1918: Germany announces an armistice

A crowd at Times Square holding up headlines reading "Germany Surrenders," on 7th November, 1918.

FAST FACT

The fabric of Europe changed after the Treaty of Versailles, and also changed states from empires into autonomous states. The League of Nations was formed and it was expected that it could work towards negotiating peace and dealing with international disputes through negotiations.

Friedrich Wilhelm riding horse statue in the Braunschweig, Germany.

HISTORY ENCYCLOPEDIA

End of the German War

Awaiting the appointment of a new chancellor, Ludendorff and Hindenburg gained the German Emperor's permission to urgently initiate peace. In his efforts, he met national political leaders and gave an update on Germany's weakening military strength. The new chancellor Prince Maximilian of Baden requested an armistice and negotiations based on Wilson's own pronouncements.

Trouble brews

The Social Democratic Party led by Friedrich Ebert was Germany's leading party. They urged Kaiser to abdicate so that Germany could be saved from its troubles. There was a fear that the extremists would take over the leadership of Germany which could lead to total anarchy. Kaiser went to Holland and on 11th November, 1918, an armistice was finally declared and the troops were asked to return.

Shortage of food

There was a severe food shortage in Germany. Farmers did not have enough young men during the harvest season because many of them had joined the army. Milk production also decreased and the supply of potatoes also reduced. It did not help that with such severe lack of food, people lacked the immunity to fight diseases like the flu. It is no wonder then that in Germany around 7,50,000 died in the war of which some lost their lives due to the flu.

Even after November, the Allies UK, France and USA maintained a food blockade to keep Germany submissive.

Disturbances in Hamburg and Bremen, the Social Democratic Party withdrawing their support from Prince Max's government and the abdication of Kaisher Wilhem's title made matters worse.

Germany becomes a republic

The Hohenzollern monarchy came to an end, just like those of the Habsburgs and Romanovs. The power was handed over to Friedrich Ebert, a Majority Social Democrat. Ebert formed a provisional government and Philipp Scheidemann, a member of the government announced that Germany was a republic.

Friedrich Ebert (1871-1925), socialist leader of the Social Democratic movement in Germany was president of the Weimar Republic from 1919 to 1925.

A bronze statue of King Maximilian Joseph of Bavaria in front of the opera in Munich, Germany.

FAST FACT

The Blockade of Germany also extended to the Central Powers of Europe. This was started in order to delay the supplies of food, raw materials and weapons to the nations of the Central Powers.

The Terms of the Armistice

The Armistice was an accord signed by representatives of France, Great Britain and Germany to agree to end fighting and work towards peace negotiations. It would be called the "Treaty of Versailles". The term "the Armistice" was used to refer to the agreement to end World War I.

Telegram read to the 5th Australian Field Ambulance by Crowther to announce the Armistice on 11th November, 1918.

Meaning of armistice

The Armistice between the Allies and Germany became an agreement that ended the fighting going on in the Western Front of Europe. Armistice comprises the Latin word "arma" meaning "arms" and "stitium", meaning "stoppage". The armistice ended the fighting, but negotiations at the 1919 Paris Peace Conference where the terms of the Treaty of Versailles were completed and signed on 28th June, 1919.

Surrender of the German Army on the Western Front, Nov 1918.

Signing of the armistice

The Armistice was signed in Ferdinand Foch's railway carriage in the Forest of Compiegne, near Paris. The World War I Armistice with Germany was signed on 11th November, 1918 by representatives from Britain, France and Germany and managed to bring more than 52 months of fighting to an end. The terms had to ensure that Germany could not restart the war. They had to give up 2,500 heavy guns, 2,500 field guns, 25,000 machine guns, 1,700 aeroplanes and all their submarines. With the signing of the Armistice and Treaty of Versailles, Germany accepted the blame for the First World War and was asked to pay reparations (compensation) for the damage caused, estimated to a total of about 22 billion pounds. While Germany thought the terms of the treaty were very harsh, the French thought they were very lenient.

FAST FACT

Did you know that Germany paid off its war debt in 2010, with a final payment of 59 million pounds?

Admiral Beatty reading the terms of the surrender of the German Navy.

World War I and the Destruction Left in its Wake

The four years' of World War I remained the worst assault on Europe. More than 85,00,000 people died, and 2,10,00,000 were wounded. The war proved to be extremely expensive. Many parts of France, Belgium and Poland lay devastated and many valuables remained destroyed at sea. It is estimated that eight million soldiers died and many more were physically or mentally affected, while nine million civilians died. The war had destroyed 3,00,000 houses, 6000 factories, 1000 km of railway lines and 112 coal mines.

Luxemburg women wave allied flags from their windows to greet the Occupation of the American Army at the end of World War I.

and became popular among revolutionaries. The war weakened the economic status that European powers had thus far enjoyed. World War I cost $186 billion in direct expenses and another $151 billion in indirect expenses. It was the first war to have employed aeroplanes, tanks, long-range artillery, submarines and poison gas, which had left at least seven million men permanently disabled. World War I brought Germany towards the brink of an economic collapse and thousands of Germans were starving. It resulted in the mutiny in the German navy. Economically, the war severely upset the European economies; thereby, making USA the chief creditor and industrial power.

Loss of life

The USA was part of World War I only for around seven and a half months. In those seven months of actual combat, close to 1,16,000 were killed and around 2,04,000 were injured. In fact, the Battle of Verdun in 1916 witnessed over a million casualties within 10 months.

Post World War I scenario

Empires had fallen and new ideologies had come forward. Woodrow Wilson had asked for new democratic diplomacy. Revolutions began in Berlin and Russia. Anti-imperialist ideas were shared

FAST FACT
A few historians believe that there was no second war. It was just one war with a long ceasefire in between!

16 soldiers leaving Camp Dix, New Jersey, in a car after 11th November, 1918.

The Axis and the Allies

The Axis alliance emerged as a result of several agreements between Germany and Italy. These were followed by the declaration of an "axis" combining Rome and Berlin, which stated that henceforth, the world would move around the Rome-Berlin axis. After this, the German-Japanese Anti-Comintern Pact against the Soviet Union was signed in 1936. Later, a complete military and political alliance was formed between Germany and Italy. Finally, all the three powers signed the Tripartite Pact on 27th September, 1940.

World War II German and American soldiers with weapons.

Old postcard showing Polish attack of Soviet tanks.

The US joins the Allies

At the beginning of World War II, Russia and Germany were on the same side, but Russia joined the Allies when Hitler ordered a surprise attack on Russia in 1941. The US wanted to be neutral during World War II, but they joined the Allies after the surprise attack at Pearl Harbor by the Japanese.

The Anti-Comintern Pact

In 1936, Germany and Italy signed a friendship treaty and established the Rome-German Axis.

The Italian dictator Benito Mussolini used the term axis to describe their alliance. Soon, Japan and Germany signed the Anti-Comintern Pact—a treaty against communism; thus, forming the Axis Powers.

In November 1936, the Foreign Minister of Germany Joachim von Ribbentrop negotiated an agreement between Germany and Japan wherein the countries openly declared opposition to international communism.

In the event of a Soviet Union attack on Germany or Japan, the two nations would discuss with each other the measures to be taken to protect their interests. They also agreed that they would not make any political treaties with Russia.

FAST FACT

Around 100 million people of the armed forces were engaged in World War II. It is considered as the most devastating war in history, in which close to 2.5 per cent of the world's population died.

World War II photo of soldier hiding and covering behind a burning jeep wreck.

US Navy F4Us, Corsairs, in flight over South Pacific in 1943, during World War II.

Outbreak of World War II

World War II began owing to the rise of authoritarian, military regimes in the states of Germany, Italy and Japan, which resulted from the Great Depression that swept across the world during 1929 and 1930. Post World War I, an overpowered Germany, disenchanted Italy, and a determined Japan were eager to regain power. These countries were against Communism. The other states were unprepared and not ready to engage in war again after World War I. It did not help that the League of Nations was weakened as the US had defected from it and the supposed union of nation states at a global level was unable to promote disarmament.

Soviet Foreign Minister Molotov signs the German-Soviet Nonaggression Pact with German Foreign Minister Joachim von Ribbentrop.

Events leading to World War II

The second Sino-Japanese War in 1931 also did not help matters as treaties were violated and states became even more aggressive. Adolf Hitler again prepared the German army. Benito Mussolini invaded and conquered Ethiopia. The Spanish civil war from 1936 to 1939 also added to the distress in Europe and both Germany and Italy helped fascist Francisco Franco win. In 1938, Germany conquered Austria and soon a British and French appeasement policy with the Axis powers ended with the handing over of Czechoslovakia to Germany as per the Munich Pact.

The Nonaggression Pact

German dictator Adolf Hitler wanted to invade and occupy Poland, which had the support of France and Britain. Soon, negotiations between Germany and Poland led to the signing of the German-Soviet Nonaggression Pact, as per which both Germany and Russia agreed that Poland will be divided between them. On 31st August, 1939 Hitler ordered his forces to invade Poland; Britain and France responded by declaring war on Germany on 3rd September and thus, the Second World War began.

Adolf Hitler, leader of Nazi Germany.

Nazi award - Knight's Cross of the Iron Cross.

Two Chinese men kneeling prior to execution by Chinese soldiers. The Sino-Japanese war (1937-1945) was a fight against the Japanese occupation of China as well as a civil war between the Nationalists and Communists in China.

WORLD WAR I

World War II Douglas Dauntless Dive-Bomber.

An old hand grenade and bullet.

World War II Weaponry

A larger number of countries were involved in World War II than in World War I. By the end of World War I, tanks and military aircraft had become a pre-requisite for a better defence and offence, due to the huge and quick destruction they caused. However, World War II was the largest armed war in human history. This period witnessed dramatic and significant scientific developments that resulted in the use of nuclear weapons in warfare for the first time.

Use of arms

By the end of World War I, the victorious Allied forces had begun to believe in their supremacy and so their pace of introducing newer weapons and artillery in their armies seemed to slow down. However, the defeated nation of Germany had started developing tanks and begun to aggressively build a better and stronger army by 1935. In stark comparison, England by 1939 had not even started work towards building an armoured division.

Aerial combat

By the end of World War I and the beginning of World War II, the use of the sky in defence tactics had also altered to a great extent. During the interim period between 1918 and 1939, the range and size of aeroplanes had developed to a considerable degree. With better speed, engine power and performance, aircrafts were slowly becoming more sophisticated. Better aircraft technology in terms of instrumentation, power-assisted flight controls and radar tracking began to emerge. These developments made use of aircrafts integral to defence and offense tactics during World War II. Dive-bombers, monoplane fighter planes, machine guns, light and medium bombers were some of the weapons employed in air warfare during World War II. Radar stations were built on the coasts of England to warn of impending attacks from hostile planes.

FUN FACT

Between 1939 and 1945, the Allies dropped around 27,700 tons of bombs per month.

Three US Navy Dauntless dive bombers on a fighting mission in the Pacific in 1943.

Vintage American M24 Tank.

Russo-Finnish War

The Russo-Finnish war, also known as Winter War, was fought between Russia and Finland. It started on 30th November, 1939 and ended on 10th March, 1940. Due to Finland's rejection of Russia's request for a naval base in 1939, Russia with a heavy force of around a million soldiers attacked Finland and the Finnish army with its smaller force put on a brave front.

Birth of the Republic of Finland

From the twelfth century to the early 1800s, Finland was a part of Sweden. Napoleon persuaded Alexander I of Russia to declare war on Sweden, and Finland became the prize of victory during that war. Finland remained a part of Russia from 1808 to 1918 under the Tsar. However, during Russia's Revolution of 1905, Finland managed to create for itself a modern, unicameral parliament with elected representatives and it also became the first European country to offer women political suffrage at the national level. By 1917, Finland declared its independence. A civil war erupted between the Red faction backed by the Soviet Bolsheviks and the Germany-backed White faction. In 1918, General Mannerheim with Germany's assistance defeated Russia. General Mannerheim established the Republic of Finland.

Carl Gustaf Emil Mannerheim (1867-1951).

Russia's foreign policy of 1939

Russia signed treaties of mutual assistance with Lithuania, Estonia and Latvia, which allowed Russia to establish military bases in all these Baltic states. In October 1939, Russia invited Finnish representatives to Moscow to discuss land issues around the Finnish/Russian border. Russia wanted certain Finnish islands in the Gulf of Finland, including Suursaari Island, in order to establish a military base. In return, Finland would get Soviet Karelia. Finland viewed Stalin's demands as an attempt by Russia to re-establish its authority over Finland, so Stalin's proposal was rejected. By the end of November 1939, a war between Finland and Russia seemed inevitable.

Frozen bodies of dead Soviet (Russian) soldiers killed in the Russo-Finnish War.

1939: Start of Russo-Finnish
1940: End of Russo-Finnish War

Dead Russian soldier covered with a dusting of snow, a casualty of the Battle of Suomussalmi, during the Russo-Finnish War of 1939-40.

Hitler's Role in World War II

Adolf Hitler became one of the most powerful and notorious dictators in history. He joined the National Socialist German Workers' Party and soon took over the reins of Germany by 1933. Hitler joined the German army and rose to the rank of corporal and despite not being popular amongst his comrades he was awarded Germany's highest award for bravery—the Iron Cross. His main job in the army was also to meet political organisations and understand their learnings—left or right.

German Nazi flag demonstrates historical reconstruction of combat between Soviet and German armies during World War II.

Adolf Hitler

Hitler's role in World War II

Hitler established several concentration camps to imprison Jews. He believed that they were a danger to Aryan superiority and this view led to the death of more than six million people in the Holocaust. Germany attacked Poland in 1939 and this sparked off World War II. By 1941, Hitler's troops had occupied much of Europe and north Africa.

Hitler's entry into the politics of Germany

Hitler evaded military service in Austria-Hungary and went to Vienna. He volunteered for the Bavarian army and served during World War I and soon became a member of the Nationalist Socialist German Workers' Party. He soon controlled the National Socialist German Workers Party and after a coup attempt and a jail sentence later, he called for the restructuring of Germany on the basis of race.

1933: Hitler heads Germany

1939: Germany attacks Poland

FUN FACT
Eva Braun, a shop assistant from Munich, became Adolf's mistress. He married her much later towards the end of his life.

Adolf Hitler in Nuremberg to attend a Nazi Party Convention in September 1934.

HISTORY ENCYCLOPEDIA

Hitler's Views on Race

As Germany's ruler for 12 years, Adolf Hitler became the reason for the deaths of many. After being recognised as a veteran for his work in World War I, he became a part of the German Workers' Party and renamed it as the National Socialist German Workers Party (in short Nazi Party). He unsuccessfully tried to overthrow the German Weimar Republic and was jailed for this. In prison, he wrote his manifesto, Mein Kampf (My Struggle), and became popular because of his strong oratory skills. By 1933, he became the Chancellor and brought in new rules.

German Chancellor, Adolf Hitler, shaking hands with a Brownshirt during the Nazi Party Day in Nuremberg, 1937.

Germany declares war on Poland

Hitler believed that Germany must wage wars to acquire land in order to enable more Germans to prosper and raise big families. By the time he came to power, Germany had started military preparations to wage such wars. He was determined to wage a war against Poland and to do so aligned with Russia. Before the full attack on Poland, German troops seized Norway in April 1940 to facilitate the navy's access to the North Atlantic. After reaching France, Hitler decided to wage wars against the US and Russia.

Hitler's War

The term Hitler's War is often used in reference to World War II because it was due to his will and push that led to the start of World War II. Hitler became infamous for his dictatorial ways and his hatred towards the Jews, which led to the construction of concentration camps where millions of people were tortured and killed.

Liberated prisoners of Wobbelin concentration camp taken to a hospital for medical attention on 4th May, 1945.

Nazi helmet

FUN FACT
Despite being the person responsible for building concentration camps that imprisoned Jews, Hitler never visited a concentration camp in his lifetime.

Entrance of Nazi flagbearers at the Party Day rally in Nuremberg, 1933.

Invasion of Norway

A few months after the start of World War II, Adolf Hitler realised that controlling the Norwegian coastal waters would be important from many perspectives, as that was how the Swedish iron ore was transported to German blast furnaces. The German occupation of Norway would prevent the entry of the Allies into Germany. Consequently, Hitler issued the order to invade Norway under the code word Weserübung, which also included the invasion of Denmark. So, Germany invaded Norway on 9th April, 1940.

German 1943 poster depicts men carrying Nazi banner going off to fight.

Germany's interest in Norway

The control of Norway's extensive coastline became important since it would mean the control of the North Sea and could provide German warships and submarines easy access to the Atlantic Ocean. Furthermore, through Norway, Germany could get easy access to importing iron ore from Sweden.

Germany occupies Denmark

By April 1940, Nazi troops were able to occupy Denmark without much of a fight. No sooner than they occupied Denmark, they made way to attack Norway. On the first day, they brought in the infantry into Norway and gained control over quite a large area of Norway.

By 15th April, English troops reached to assist the Norwegian forces, but a strong attack by the German forces forced the English troops to flee Norway.

Further, the German troops were able to slip through the mines that the English forces had laid near Norwegian ports. This was possible as local garrisons had been commanded to permit Germans to enter, under the orders of a Norwegian commander loyal to Norway's pro-fascist former foreign minister Vidkun Quisling.

Heavy fire from German troops led to a hasty evacuation of 360,000 Allied troops from Dunkirk to England.

German soldiers invade Poland in armoured and motorised divisions in September 1939. It was the beginning of World War II.

Monument for Soviet soldiers in Kirkenes city, Norway who liberated northern Norway from Nazi occupation in 1944.

HISTORY ENCYCLOPEDIA

The German Attack

German forces, led by Erwin Rommel, struck at the weak extension at Maginot Line in the Ardennes Forest and succeeded. Both attacks met quick success. Norway with a population of three million and a small population meant a smaller army. While the German occupation attempt was relatively successful, it was not without its glitches, because the Norwegian forces managed to sink Germany's new cruiser called *SMS Blucher* at Oslo. This act gave the forces some time to delay the German possession of the capital Helsinki and also gave an opportunity to the members of the Norwegian royal family and government to escape.

The German armoured cruiser SMS Blücher, launched on 11th April, 1908 and sunk at the battle of Dogger Bank on 24th January, 1915.

Germany invades Norway

Just after Germany invaded Norway, there was a demand for Norway's surrender, but the Norwegian government rejected this demand. So, the German troops established another regime under Quisling. Soon after the invasion, a German minister in Oslo demanded that Norway surrender. The Norwegian government did not accept and the Germans responded with a parachute invasion, and the establishment of a puppet regime under Quisling. The Norwegian forces rejected Germany's rule in the guise of a Quisling government and continued fighting along with British troops.

General Rommel standing in a jeep in the North African desert. Rommel's German-Italian forces were supplied tanks and fuel in January 1942. He soon captured Benghazi, Libya.

Effects of the German invasion of Norway

The economic impact of the German invasion resulted in Norway losing all its major trading partners, resulting in Germany becoming its main trading partner. Germany confiscated a major portion of Norway's output and left Norway with around 43 per cent of it. Norway faced scarcity of basic commodities, including food. There was an increased risk of famine so the Norwegians grew crops to feed themselves.

German soldiers in Frederikshavn, Denmark, before being sent to Norway.

Swastika armband from World War II.

FUN FACT

Quisling soon became a word synonymous with traitor, owing to Quisling's siding with Germany in World War II.